Sometimes I'm a Fire-Breathing Dragon

Dedicated to the real Caleb, Maia and Jack. Thanks for the inspiration.

Sometimes I'm a Fire-Breathing Dragon
Copyright © 2010 by Kelsea Parks Wierenga
All rights reserved.
Summary: Three siblings learn how to deal with their feelings with a little help from their imaginations.
The text of this book is set in 16 pt Hank BT. The illustrations are mixed media.
ISBN: 0-615-32178-X  EAN-13: 978-0-615-32178-3
[Juvenile Fiction —Imagination & Play.]

Seesaw Publishing
Charleston, South Carolina

# Sometimes I'm a Fire-Breathing Dragon

## A Story about Feelings

Kelsea Parks Wierenga

Mom comes to the rescue and gives my train back to me. "You know, it's not nice to blow fire at your sister," she says. But she takes Maia to the kitchen for a snack so that I can keep playing.

Maia has just decided on cereal when— "Hello there, little one!" ...says a lady with a shopping bag.

Sometimes Maia feels **scared** when a stranger talks to her.

She feels so **scared**, she imagines that...

Today is my birthday. I am tons bigger than I was last year! But sometimes I feel shy when everyone sings to me.

Dad says that people like to sing the happy birthday song because they are happy that I was born.

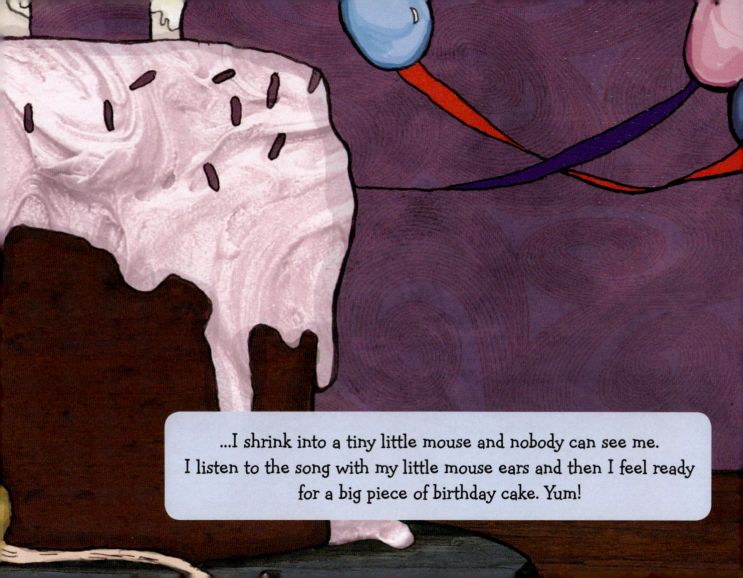

Made in the USA
Lexington, KY
17 March 2016